$0 to Six Figures

A Writer's Guide to
Financial Success

Teresa Burrell

Dedication

To my dear friend, author Jeff Sherratt. Thank you for holding my hand and leading me through a rough beginning in the publishing world. I miss your guiding hand, your sense of humor, and the great stories you always told about your life. Rest in peace, my friend.

Acknowledgments

A huge thank you to my team:

L.J. Sellers
Madeline Settle
Victoria Showalter
Robin Thomas

Table of Contents

Prelude

Who Should Read This Book?

If your dream is to make a living as an author—you can. I wrote this book because I believe it's okay for writers to make a living at their craft. I know that sounds obvious, but some writers don't believe in their own self-worth and/or the value of the books they write. You do not need to be a starving artist. It is okay to profit from your art.

This guide is not about a quick fix. It's a legitimate way to build your book-selling business. It takes work, but the payoff is worth it.

Most people dream of writing a book someday. Everyone has a story to tell. Each life is different; we have all experienced joy, and no one escapes tragedy. Those are the things that make for an interesting read. It is your job to find a way to use your life's experiences to weave a tale. If you do, someone will want to read it. But that's not the type of author this book is written for. This how-to guide is for the person who loves to write, has to write to feel complete, and would like to turn their passion for writing into a career.

Have a good look at your writing goals. This book is not for the *one-trick pony*. It's for the serious writer. If that's you, read on. This is not about how to write a best-seller, make millions of dollars, and retire. Perhaps you will, but most likely, you won't. This is for the dedicated writer who is willing to keep writing even when things are not working. The writer who is willing to put in the time and effort it takes to market their book so the world can experience it.

The title implies authors can earn a six-figure income. The following pages are filled with a road map for how I did just that. Does that mean *you* can make a six-figure income as a writer? That depends. There are lots of variables to the process I have outlined here, not the least of which is what kind of writer you are. I can't control those variables, but for the most part, you can.

I initially named this book *$0 to Six Figures in Seven Not-So-Easy Steps*. I changed it because the title was too long to fit on the cover and make it esthetically appealing. The seven steps are still there, and you need to do them all, but start by putting your effort into Step 1. If you can't master that step, the others won't work either.

Some genres may work better than others. Will it work with poetry? I don't know. I've never tested it, but whatever your genre, I expect if you follow the steps, you'll do better than you are doing now without them.

I've had several careers in my lifetime. First I was a teacher, then a lawyer, a businesswoman, and now an author. Each of these careers has helped me as a writer, and I enjoyed every one of them, but nothing is as rewarding as making a living doing what you love. If your passion is writing, then hopefully, this book will help you attain your goals.

Chapter 1

Step 1—Write a Good Book

The first step is to write a good book with good characters, if it's fiction, or good information, if it's non-fiction. It doesn't have to be the great American novel, but it does have to be good enough that readers will not want to put it down once they start reading. And when it is finished, they'll want to read another book that you have written. They will develop loyalty to you as an author and to whatever else you have to offer.

This book is not just about writing; it's about starting a new career, a new business—the business of writing. I can't stress that enough, because this *is* a business, and it must be treated as such if you want to make money at it. So how do you do that? You start by hiring an editor.

Edit the Manuscript

When I say, "Write a good book," I not only mean a book with good content, but also without grammatical errors. This means you need to have professional eyes look at it. You cannot edit your own work. I'll repeat that, in case you didn't hear me. YOU CANNOT EDIT YOUR OWN WORK. Yes, you need to edit and possibly re-write the story several times before you send it to an editor, but then you must have it edited by someone with editorial experience. That does not mean your high school English teacher, or your very smart spouse. Well, you can have them go through it too, but then you still need to have it professionally edited.

There is some cost involved, but in the long run, you'll be glad you did it. Editors charge anywhere from a couple hundred dollars per book to thousands. Keep in mind, you usually get what you pay for. Try to get referrals from other writers. Then preview the editor's work and determine if it will be a good fit for you. Using an editor who was referred to you keeps you from going in blindly. Most editors are willing to edit a page or two as a sample. Take advantage of that. Try them on and see how they fit before you spend a lot of money.

Some editors charge by the word, others use an hourly rate, and some go by page count. This may take a little research to find the best fit within your budget, but you haven't finished Step 1 until you have your book professionally edited.

While you're searching for an editor, be mindful that there are two kinds of editors: content and copy. You may need both. I'll talk more about editing a little later for those who decide to self-publish. I mention it here, because if your book is traditionally published, they will edit it again. That does not mean you can write a draft, submit it to an agent or publisher, and let them edit it. If there are too many errors, agents and publishers will stop reading and chances are you won't get a book deal. Do not think your book is so unique and such a good story that once it's read, everyone will want it. That's not the way it works. If it's riddled with mistakes, it won't ever get read, so no one will ever know how good it is.

Now that you have a well-written book, what's next? You have to decide whether you want to try to get a publisher or go the Independent route and self-publish.

Traditional Publishers

So far in my writing career, I have had two traditional publishers, and I have also self-published. There are advantages and disadvantages to both. Deciding which way to go is a personal decision that depends on your goals. If you've done a good job on Step 1, you *can* find a traditional publisher if you want to. However, it does not guarantee you will land a contract with one of the big-five publishers—Penguin/Random House, Harper-Collins, Simon & Schuster, Hatchette Book Group, or Macmillan.

I want to point out a misconception. I often hear writers brag about getting published, only to find out they paid someone to publish their book. That is not traditional publishing. There may be a place for that kind of publishing, but those presses don't pick you because you're the best writer. They produce your book because you pay the fees for their service. For some people it works, but do not confuse that method with traditional publishing, and do not expect a lot of help with marketing. Traditional publishing means they pay you an advance and you receive royalties from them as the book sells.

There are thousands of small and medium publishing houses looking for good books. I'm not talking about vanity presses that you pay. I'm talking about publishers who pay you to take your book, edit it, format it, create a cover, and pay you an advance. Those advances are generally quite small, but the point is they pay you—you don't pay them. They can be a great way to get started. The problem is that the small presses don't have a lot of money to spend on promoting your books, so you will still need to do a lot of marketing.

Some new hybrid houses have popped up that may also work for you. Hybrid publishing is an emerging style that falls somewhere between traditional and self-publishing. I heard one company refer to it as "guided self-publishing." Most of these companies will provide fee-based services, which can include edits, cover design, formatting, and some marketing. A few of these businesses use their imprint (publishing label) instead of yours. Some may have the ability to get you shelf space in bookstore, and others have no connections whatsoever. Some are just vanity presses with an innovative name. Do your research and make certain the company is a good choice for you.

One test for a hybrid publisher is: Will they take just anyone for a fee? If so, they are probably a vanity press. You should read some of the books the press puts out before you sign on the dotted line. Make sure what they are publishing is good quality.

Large publishing houses do not accept submissions without an agent, so if you plan to go the traditional route, you will need to obtain an agent. They are the gatekeepers who sort through thousands of daily submissions before they ever get to the publishers. If your goal is to get an agent, you need to put in the time it takes. You must peruse the agents' lists, which can be obtained online. Read what they are looking for, and do not submit to them if they do not cover your genre. Don't think you'll be able to convert them because you have written the best book ever, because chances are they won't even read your manuscript. The agents themselves receive hundreds of query letters every week. The writers who have not followed their submission requirements are not going to get their material read. It's as simple as that.

When you're querying agents, keep in mind that your letter is the first thing they'll see from you. If it isn't well written, or doesn't follow their submission requirements, or if it contains typos, they'll stop reading. Your query letter must reflect your writing. Learn how to write a good one, then have it edited before you send it.

Even though traditional publishing takes longer and isn't guaranteed, it has benefits that may make it worth pursuing.

Store Placement

Traditional publishers can make your books available for brick-and-mortar bookstores. That does not mean your books will be on their shelves. It just means they can order them and put them on their shelves if they choose to. Most bookstores do not stock work by new writers. The stores are filled with best-selling books and new novels by major publishers who pay dearly for the best promotional displays.

Bookstore Events

If you want to have a book signing event in bookstores, it's important that store managers can get your books through a distributor, which is easier when you have a traditional publisher. The stores need to be able to order your books and return them if they don't sell. Sometimes you can get a store manager to let you bring in your own books on consignment. They sell the books, let you have a signing event, and take a percentage of the sales, usually about 40%. This is more likely to happen with an independent bookstore than a major chain.

It's important to note that just having a book in a store does not mean you'll get a book-signing gig. I've been told by managers that most of the unknown authors who do book signings sell between five and ten books, which are usually purchased by friends who have shown up to support the author.

Even self-published authors can get book signings in stores—it just takes a lot more work. Some major bookstores have a small-press department that handles these authors. As an independent publisher, or if you're with a small press, you can fill out the necessary forms, plead your case, and maybe get in. Once you get in, you'd better sell some books because otherwise, you will not be invited back.

Independent bookstores are more apt to allow you in

for a book signing, but you still need to make a good showing. If you are able to secure one of those spots, make sure you get as many of your friends as you can to attend. The reason the store is willing to give you the opportunity is because they're hoping you'll bring a crowd and increase their sales.

Independent Publishing

Independent publishing is also known as self-publishing. If you decide to self-publish, you should have already invested some money in your work. You should have had it edited, which is probably the most significant cost to pre-publishing. If you haven't had your manuscript edited by a professional—do it now. It is an absolute must. You cannot skip having your book professionally edited, especially if you decide to self-publish. Let's talk about that for a bit.

Editing

I cannot stress enough what an important part of the process this is. Do NOT use your spouse or someone close to you as your final editor. They can help get your book into shape before you send it to a professional, but if you think they can edit as well as an independent source, you will be sadly disappointed.

Did you know readers can report errors to Amazon, and that Amazon will, in response, contact the author or publisher and tell them to fix the errors? I personally think that's a good thing, but if you get too many of them, Amazon can remove your book from the marketplace. If you already have books on Amazon and have never received one of these emails, you may think your book is perfect, but that typically isn't the case. More than likely the lack of emails asking for corrections is because your book hasn't been read by enough people. Someone will find a mistake if enough people are reading it—even after it's professionally edited. They just won't find as many.

So, how do you find an editor? As with anything else, you can Google it. You'll turn up tons, but just like any other profession, there are some who are better than others. If you're on social media (and if you're not, you should be), reach out to your author friends and ask for referrals. I don't need to explain the benefits of getting a referral over hiring someone you know nothing about. It is not different than finding the right person to paint your house or groom your dog.

There are also hundreds, if not thousands, of forums that cater to writers. Start your search for an editor by determining the genre in which you write. Join a few forums, or Facebook groups, and start to interact. At the very least, it's good practice for what's to come.

The three experts you will need to self-publish a book are: an editor, a book formatter, and a cover designer. Don't be afraid to ask other writers who they use for these services. If you choose, you can format and design your own book; however, as I've mentioned, I absolutely do not recommend editing the book yourself. As the author, you already know what is supposed to be on the page, which means your brain will likely read it as it's supposed to appear rather than as it actually does, often resulting in mistakes that are overlooked.

Once your book is edited, and you have made all the corrections, you can have others proofread it for final typos and other minor errors. Because even the best editors can overlook missing words, and multiple proofreaders will find different mistakes. You can use friends and family at first, but after you have a following, it's a good idea to ask your readers to do this for you. These readers are often referred to as *beta readers*.

Beta Readers

Beta readers can be used in many different capacities. Some writers have them read the manuscript before it's edited to look for holes in the storyline. You can have them fact check, look for inconsistent details such as eye color, and make sure the characters haven't switched cars or names mid-book. Other writers use their beta readers in the capacity of proofreaders who look for misplaced punctuation, missing words, or typos. Whatever your need, be sure to convey it to your readers. Give them detailed instructions on what you want done.

How do you find these beta readers? As I mentioned, at first you may need to use friends and family. Once you get a following, you will discover readers who can't wait to get your next book. These readers are typically more than willing to read the book before it is published. Of course, if you're asking someone to beta read, you need to give them a free copy of your manuscript.

I receive a lot of emails from my readers. In the beginning, some were very critical and pointed out errors in my books. (I had more errors when I first started because I hadn't mastered this process.) I always asked those critical readers to become beta readers for me—because they already had an eye for proofing. Most have since become fans. That can be a problem though, because once they become fans of your writing, they often get caught up in the story and don't read with such a critical eye. For that reason, you have to constantly update your beta reader list. But don't forget about those who helped you when you first started. If they want to keep proofreading for you, let them. I use about fifteen readers for each book, and most find different mistakes.

Formatting

There are basically two kinds of book formatting— eBook formatting, which is html and needs to flow, and print book formatting, which is more like printing a picture. If you hire it done, you will likely need to pay for both, which will be separate files. However, book formatting is something you can learn to do yourself. I know because I learned to do it, and I'm not that technologically sophisticated. Please do NOT just upload your manuscript to Kindle Publishing, Smashwords, or any of the other publishing places, and expect it to be correctly formatted. It is not that simple. If you are not confident in your ability to format your book yourself, hire someone to do it for you. It's not that expensive to have it done. Again, talk to others who have gone before you and find out who they use.

If you want to put your formatting dollars into marketing instead—and you have a good grasp of computer software—you can learn to format yourself. I know it can be done, because that's the way I started. I was fortunate enough to have a friend, Jeff Sherratt, who had learned the process and gave me some pointers. Back then, it was the best choice for me because I had way more time than money, which was a good thing, because it took me many, many hours and lots of failures to learn the eBook formatting process. After I finally mastered it, I only formatted a couple of my own books because I decided I needed the time for writing. Now I have it done by a professional.

Cover Design

Book cover design is similar to book formatting in that you can do it yourself or hire a professional. I recommend the latter. Your cover is the first thing the reader sees. This is the first chance you get to make an impression, and if it isn't a good one, you may not get a second chance. The cover has to catch the eye of the reader and look professional, not only in paperback form, but more importantly in thumbnail size. For most of your ebook readers, the thumbnail size is all they will ever see. More and more books are sold online both in print and digital forms, and only a few minutes, or even seconds, are all many potential sales get. Thanks to the internet and technology, purchases are made much quicker than they used to be. People do not spend nearly as much time perusing as they might in a bookstore. They cannot pick up the book and handle it, so it's even more important that the first impression is powerful.

Don't ignore the back cover. It is almost as important as the front. You should have a concise description of your book, no more than a paragraph or two, a couple of review quotes by recognizable names (if you can get them), and a professional photo with a short bio. All of this must be error free. If there are errors anywhere on your cover, chances are, the book will not be purchased, let alone opened and read.

You can create your own cover or hire a book designer. Doing it yourself requires some knowledge of graphic design and proficiency in graphic-art programs. I had neither, so I obtained referrals from my writer friends and have worked with a few excellent cover designers.

Go back to the forums or your Facebook groups and find out who they use.

Pricing

This is an important step. If you price your book too high, few will buy it, and you won't make much money. If you price it too low, more people will buy it, but you won't make much money. What do you do? The answer depends on several factors. Do you have one book or a series of novels? Do you want to make a living from writing, or is this the only book you plan to write? If your book is non-fiction, do you plan to use it for some purpose other than mere entertainment or imparting knowledge, such as lining up speaking events? Is this a picture book for children?

Let's assume you're reading this advice because you plan to write your first book. Unless you get lucky, this is just the first phase in a long line of many. Every writer, including myself, started with one book, so I know what it's like. You finish the book. You have it edited. You may even have a publisher. You have it posted in Amazon and in Barnes & Noble's online store. Perhaps it's even in a few local bookstores. You're ready to set the world on fire with sales. You sit back and wait for the money to roll in, but no one buys your book, except a few close friends and family.

How does this happen? Your book is great. Everyone should want to read it. The truth is, there are millions of other books out there to choose from and no one knows about yours. You have to bring it to readers' attention. I'll talk more about marketing in a later chapter.

Various Formats

There are several different formats in which your work can be published. There is print form, digital, and audio. It's important that you do all three to maximize your earning potential.

Print

Your book needs to be in print. First, it feels really good to see and handle your physical book. If for no other reason, it will boost your confidence. Once you have it, you can place it on your shelf and look at it every day. Soon you will discover there are other reasons to have a print version, especially since it gives you some credibility—with certain readers and industry professionals—that you may not get with a digital book.

You also need the printed book for signing events. As part of your marketing plan, it is important to make public appearances. If they like your writing, the readers you meet will stay with you throughout your career. Once they know you, they have more reasons to read your work because they like more than your book. They like *you,* and they want to support *you.*

When you make public appearances, which we will talk about later, you need a physical book to sign. Readers love to meet authors. If you are friendly and genuine and offer something they want, you will create lifelong fans.

If you want to get your book into stores, you obviously need a print version. I spent the first three years of my novelist career, almost every weekend, standing in bookstores from Friday morning until Sunday night, doing meet-and-greets and signing books. Yes, I said *standing*. You cannot meet and greet people from your chair. This is true of most events you will do. I'll get into this in more depth in a later chapter.

Digital

Even more important than print is the digital version. This is where I make the majority of my money. You absolutely must have digital copies if you are trying to make a living as a writer. When I say you must be digital, at the very least, you need to make your book available on Amazon's Kindle. There are other digital distributors, such as Nook, Barnes & Noble's digital reader, and Kobo, which is well-known internationally.

One of the most important questions writers face is, do you go exclusive with Amazon by signing up for Kindle Direct Publishing Select (aka KDP Select) or diversify and use other digital venues? With most businesses, diversifying is generally the best way to go.

However, the book-selling business is different. Amazon offers certain perks when you are exclusive to them. One is Kindle Unlimited, an eBook subscription service that allows readers to borrow up to ten books at a time. Authors are paid for each page read when these books are borrowed. With some of my books, I actually make more when they are borrowed and read than when they are purchased. Most months, I make more on borrowed books than I do on sales.

Another perk Kindle Select offers is the countdown deal. With this deal, you can discount your book in increments for up to seven days, but you get to keep the same royalty structure. Using Kindle Select also allows you to offer your book for free for five days in each ninety-day enrollment period. However, if you enroll in Kindle Select, you cannot offer your eBook for sale with any other retailer or service provider.

Many authors recommend that you do not use Kindle Select or go exclusive with Amazon. I have tried both— exclusive to Amazon and a wider distribution—and in my personal experience, I made a lot more money using the Select program. Before deciding, you need to do your own research and see what works best for you. That said, the book market is constantly changing. Kindle Select does not produce the same level of financially benefits that it used to, partly because Amazon has changed the way its algorithms work. Don't be afraid to experiment to find what works best for you.

Audio

If you already have your book in print and in digital formats, why not create an audio version too? You've already done all the hard work, and if you don't produce it in audio form, you're leaving money on the table.

How do you make an audio version of your book? There are many ways. Some are costly and some are not. You can hire a narrator, go to a studio, and create the book with your constant input on how the lines are read. You can have CDs made and try to market them yourself. This method is expensive and not one I would recommend unless you have unlimited funds and absolutely need to have a copy of your book on CD.

There are ways to create an audio book without any cost to you. One is through Audio Creation Exchange, or ACX.com, Amazon's streaming service. The final product will appear on Audible.com and on Amazon. Again, you have choices, depending on how much you want to invest. You can do your own recording if you have the skills and the equipment. You can also go to a studio and record yourself reading the book, then have them upload the final product to ACX. You can hire an outside narrator and have them upload the final product to ACX. I rented a studio and hired a narrator for my first book. It wasn't my best move, even though I make a higher royalty on Audible.com for that book than I do from the others. Going that route was expensive and time consuming, even though I did have a fun experience and learned a lot. Although I don't think I would do that again, I know lots of authors who've had great experiences and found independent professional recording to be the best way to go.

The simplest way to create an audio book is to sign up on ACX and hire a professional narrator to record your book. You can pay them an hourly rate, or you can do a royalty split with the narrator with no upfront cost to you. I have tried both ways. Earlier, when I wasn't making as much money on sales, I did a royalty split. Now, I usually pay the narrator upfront and collect the full royalty, minus what Amazon keeps. The point is, you can make money on the audio version without any out-of-pocket costs.

To use ACX, you will upload a page or so of your manuscript and ask for auditions. If you don't get the auditions you want, you can listen to various narrators' samples and reach out to them. Some will sound terrible to you, others will be great. Just keep at it until you find the one you want. You are the final decision maker and must find a voice you like for your book.

When you work with the narrator, you get final say on how it is done. I go through each chapter after it has been narrated and follow along with my book. If I hear a mistake in pronunciation or the wrong emphasis on something, I simply send an email to the narrator and he or she fixes it. You have complete control.

This is time well spent. I have sold just under ten thousand audio books and have made tens of thousands of dollars through this avenue. Don't dismiss it lightly.

~ ~ ~

Step 1: Write A Good Book—Bottom Line

No matter which avenue you take to publishing, you must have a well-written book, free of grammatical and typographical errors. This must all be done before you submit the manuscript to an agent or publisher. If you choose to publish your book independently, you must complete all of the above before the public sees it.

Chapter 2

Step 2—Create an Audience

Note that I didn't say *create an email list*. A readership is way more than that. You must create an audience, not just a list of people you can contact. What's the difference? Your livelihood. Anyone can maintain a long mailing list, but to have an audience, you must build a list of readers who are interested in your books, or at the very least, your genre. You must communicate. You must be genuine. And you must care about your readers. You want real readers, not just names and addresses. Here's how you do that.

Email Marketing Services

These programs allow you to create and manage your email list, then send friendly updates to your readers. They are a good way to build your brand. It is an absolute MUST to use one of these services. You can create your own email system if you have the skills, but I certainly don't, so I signed up with a service. You need a program that allows you to easily identify a reader's location, likes, or special groups. You need to be able to communicate with your entire list on a regular basis. Paying a monthly stipend to an established email marketing service is the easiest way to do it.

There are several email services available, some for free, some for a price. The cost is usually determined by the size of your list. AWeber, Constant Contact, Mad Mimi, MailChimp, and MailerLite are just a few.

I used several of these until I found the one that worked best for me, which at the time of this writing is MailerLite. Some companies have a free trial for a short period of time. Others offer a free trial up to a certain number of subscribers, which range from one to two thousand. Some allow an unlimited number of emails per month while others stop at 12,000. If you start with the free membership, by the time you reach the point where the service requires payment, hopefully you will be making enough money to afford the service. Check the cost because the prices vary quite a bit as your list grows.

Some programs are more user friendly than others. Depending on your skill level, this could be another factor to consider. Some offer better updates and improvements to their service. Make certain the service you choose offers an auto-responder because that will save you a lot of time in the long run. Auto-responders are a way to send out messages to your list automatically. For example, when someone signs up to receive your newsletter, a pre-designed email will go out to them within a minute or an hour or two (whatever time schedule you put it on). You can also set up a follow up email campaign that goes out the next day, or the next week. This saves you from having to respond to every new fan, saying the same thing over and over again.

I used three different services until I found the one I liked best. I would suggest you check out the different mail marketing services, do your research, and see which one works best for you.

Build an Email List

This is the single most important thing you can do to maintain your readership—because it is the one thing you have complete control over. After writing the book, everything else—sales, ads, promotions—is controlled by someone else. To make money, you *must* build a large list of readers, but just having the list isn't enough. It must be comprised of actual readers. Everyone on your list should have read something you've written. It could be a short story, or your first novel, or every book you've penned. You want to avoid creating a list of people who joined just because you promised them a free Amazon gift card or some other gimmick. If they joined because you gave them a free copy of your book or short story you have written, then they are more apt to be legitimate readers.

How do you build and grow a legitimate list? Here are some ways I do it.

Festivals

There are plenty of book festivals across the United States and in other countries as well. I know of festivals in England, Scotland, India, Germany, and Brazil. I would expect there to be many in other countries that I'm not aware of. I haven't done much research into foreign festivals, but they are easy to find if you Google them. I have writer friends who have attended some of these foreign festivals and have had great success at them.

One of the largest events in the U.S. is the Los Angeles Times Festival of Books. I have participated several times. In recent years, it has become more costly than some of the others for independent authors, but it attracts more than 100,000 attendees each year.

Other book festivals I've attended include Printer's Row Lit Fest (Chicago), South Carolina Book Festival,

Southern Festival of Books (Nashville), AJC Decatur Book Festival (Atlanta), Bay Area Book Fest, San Diego Festival of Books, and Tucson Festival of Books, the latter of which I attend every year. I suggest you find the closest book fest and give it a try. Some of the events have single tables you can rent, others have booths. More often than not, you'll be able to find other authors to share the cost and keep it affordable.

Your purpose for participating in a book festival is to build your readership, not necessarily to sell books. If you can build your list by selling your print copies or promoting your eBooks, all the better. Book festivals are a great way to get acquainted with readers. Even if they don't buy something from you at the time, they likely will later. The most important element is to get their email address so you can communicate with them.

Once you meet a reader and get to know him or her, the rest is up to your book. If you have a good book, they will buy most everything else you write, because now they have an interest in both you and your writing. To establish rapport with readers, be friendly and informative, but most of all, be yourself.

Book Signings

There are numerous places you can do book signings. You just have to look around and keep asking. Let's start with the most obvious: bookstores.

Most new writers dream of signing books in a store. You envision long lines and a buzz of excitement as readers clamber to get a moment with you—the famous author. For most of us, it doesn't happen that way. The community relations managers (CRMs) at bookstores know that crowds don't come easily, which makes it difficult to even set up an event. The CRMs know that new authors without name recognition will only sell a handful of books. Consequently, they're not willing to risk their time. It is also more difficult, but not impossible, to get a book signing if you are an independent author. It's also challenging if you are published with a small press. However, some bookstores have an independent/small-press department that you can contact. Which is how I got established with Barnes & Noble.

My first book was published by a small press, and I was adamant about signing in stores. My publisher suggested that I send a letter to the small press department at both Barnes & Noble and Borders, so I did. They accepted me, and I thought the battle was over, but it had only begun. The hard part was yet come. Next, I had to convince the individual CRMs that they needed me. I went to numerous local bookstores, talked to managers, and was rejected time and again. I was fortunate enough to know a fellow writer who was willing to help me out. Jeff Sherratt and I were published by the same small press and met at the Southern California Writers Conference in San Diego. Jeff suggested I try a new bookstore and gave me ideas for how to approach it. It worked.

How I Became the Queen of Bookstore Signings

I went into a bookstore I hadn't been to before, introduced myself to the CRM, and asked her to put me on the calendar for a meet-and-greet. There are two kinds of signing events at bookstores. One is when the store invites a writer to speak or perhaps do a reading. The other is called a meet-and-greet. I didn't want to give a group talk, and I didn't want the CRM to incur the extra expense of snacks or to have to make special arrangements. All I wanted was a table near the door and for the bookstore to make copies available for purchase. The CRM explained that new writers were lucky if they sold five books at a meet-and-greet so it was a waste of time. I asked her to give me a chance. I told her I would show up Friday morning and stay till Sunday evening. And that if she ordered a hundred books, I would sell them all. She laughed. So I took out my credit card, handed it to her, and said, "If I don't sell them all, I'll buy back at retail value whatever is left. That way, you'll still make the same amount of money as if I had sold them to customers."

She looked at me like I was a little crazy. I probably was since I had no idea if I could actually sell that many books.

But she smiled and responded, "If you're that confident, I'm willing to give you a chance, but I'll only order twenty books. We'll set a date for a Saturday at 11 o'clock, and you stay until they are sold. Please don't be too disappointed if they don't sell."

I showed up on the prearranged date and asked to be near the front door. She set up a small table with my twenty books and gave me a chair. I never sat down. I had no signage of any kind for that first event, but customers had to pass near my table as they came into the store. When they did, I approached them and introduced myself. Two hours later my twenty books were sold. The CRM was pleasantly surprised, and so was I. She gave me another date about two months later, ordered a hundred books, and let me start on Friday this time. Over the next three years, I did events at that store about every six months.

I asked the CRM to write a recommendation so I could get into other Barnes & Noble stores. She emailed me a lovely letter and told other CRMs what I had accomplished, which helped me set up events in other stores. But I still had to prove myself at each new store. I got comments such as, "But this is a different clientele, it won't work here." Or, "It's easy to sell near the beach, but this is the desert." Sometimes it took a while, but I did a meet-and-greet in nearly every Barnes & Noble and Borders in Southern California. I even had some in northern California, Nevada, and Arizona.

One CRM ordered a hundred books but said I had to

sell every last one if I ever wanted to come back. He was quite serious, and even though I wasn't sure he would stick to his threat, I wasn't willing to take a chance. Determined to sell the books, I started early on the scheduled weekend, and by seven o'clock Sunday night I had sold 98 copies. I was concerned the last two books wouldn't sell because it was late and few people were coming into the store. I was tired and still had an hour-and-a-half drive home. Just then a woman, likely in her late seventies or early eighties, stopped at my table. She told me how much she loved mysteries, especially legal suspense, and what a fan she was of Erle Stanley Gardner. She held one of my books for a while, then looked in her purse and laid it back down. She said she loved the smell of new books and that owning them was a special treat to her. Then she explained she was on a fixed income and had to limit herself to buying only one book a month. The rest she checked out at the library. Her budget wouldn't allow her to purchase the book at that moment.

I found this woman so endearing that I wanted her to have a copy. So I explained my circumstances and sympathized with hers. I said, "If she would allow me, I will purchase a book for you, which would be doing me a big favor." A gentleman who was standing near us overheard the conversation and came to the table. He asked the woman her name, then asked me to sign a book for her and the other for him. She waited with me while he paid for the books. My one hundred copies were sold, and I went home a happy camper.

I continued to schedule events all throughout Southern California, Northern California, Nevada, Arizona, and a few other states where I had friends or family to stay with. For the next three years, I signed in bookstores almost every weekend from Friday morning to Sunday night and every day between Thanksgiving and Christmas Eve. I sold a lot of print books, earned very little money, and made one really big mistake. I did not yet understand the importance of gathering emails. As a result, it wasn't until part way into year three that I started to collect email addresses. And even though I still have some of my original readers—I know because I still hear from them—I've lost many more because I wasn't able to communicate with them.

The lesson here is to ask for email addresses wherever you go, whatever you do, whenever you get a book into a reader's hands. Those readers are legitimate fans, and those emails will be the sustenance of your livelihood.

The Sale—PSST

There are dozens of how-to books about selling, and if you've never sold anything, it might be worthwhile to read what the experts have to say. I'm not an expert in this field. I only know what works for me.

How do I sell a hundred books in one event to complete strangers? First, I knew enough about sales to know that I needed to sell myself. I had to be friendly, be courteous, and be me. I knew I only had a few minutes to make the sale, and if the buyer didn't like me, it wouldn't matter what I was selling or how good it might be.

I developed a technique I call PSST, which seemed an appropriate acronym because it's a way of quietly getting noticed. I don't actually say "psst" when I'm trying to get a customer's attention, but I don't approach them aggressively either. It's important to speak in a normal tone, yet make sure you get their attention. Then I start the PSST process: profile, sell, sign, tell.

Profile: Yes, profiling can be a good thing when you're selling. The dictionary defines profiling as "the use of personal characteristics or behavior patterns to make generalizations about a person." That's exactly what I do. You typically only have a few seconds to make contact when customers come near your table. If an individual approaches, it's easy—talk to him or her. The issue is when a *group* walks by. When there Is more than one person, you must determine who to talk to. Obviously, you want to approach the person most likely to buy your book. Sometimes, they sort themselves out, and the interested person (or people) starts talking to you or looking at your books. If not, you have to catch their attention.

Let's start with the most obvious—children. You aren't going to sell books to children, so you don't start with them. That doesn't mean you should be rude to anyone. You can still say hello, but do not engage because, if you do, you'll miss the potential buyers. If I have to choose between a man and a woman, I generally speak to the woman because my research indicates that women buy more than 70% of the books. Again, it doesn't mean you should ignore men. And you certainly can't decide who to talk to based on how someone is dressed or their ethnicity. If someone approaches your table, you give the best customer service you can. And never, ever stop talking to a customer because someone else walks up, no matter if the new person seems to be a more-likely buyer. If you do, you will likely lose both of them.

Once you have their attention, you need to assess the person and move on from those who don't seem interested. Please do it quickly for your sake and for theirs. Most customers likely did not come to the store or festival to see you. They have a life, and most are on a mission, so don't be long-winded. More important, you don't have time to spend chatting with people who have no interest in your genre. You're not going to convert anyone. If you meet someone who says they only read nonfiction or science fiction, chances are they're not going to read your romance novel. Start the conversation with something that determines the genres they prefer. Ask, "Do you read romance novels?" Or, "Are you a science fiction reader?" If they say "no," thank them, and move on. If they say "yes," give them a brief description or comment about your book. And I mean *brief*. I usually hand them the book. Once they have it in their hands, it's harder to give back. Also, if they're holding the book, they often read the blurb on the back. In this case, wait in silence until they're finished. Do NOT talk to your prospective buyer while they're reading.

Sell: For those brief descriptions, you need to have several one-liners ready to pitch. If you can come up with something interesting, possibly humorous, that captures your personality as well, you'll have even more success. This takes time and practice. You pitch the lines one at a time and let your reader react. Here are some lines I use for my first book:

—*My main character's name is Sabre Orin Brown. Her initials are S.O.B.*
—*This story was inspired by an actual case I was involved in. But it has been fictionalized, of course.*
—*This book has over 1800 reviews on Amazon, so someone besides my family likes it.*
—*The Advocate recently received a Reader's Favorite award.*
—*It's a similar style to John Grisham, only my lawyer can beat his lawyer.*

If they still appear interested, you have to ask for the sale. This is the one thing I have seen so many writers fail to do. You're there to sell your books, so don't be afraid to close the deal. There are subtle ways to get it done, such as:

—I'd be glad to sign a book for you.
—Who would you like me to sign this to?
—If you buy the book and don't like it, send me an email, and I'll refund your money.

If you've written a decent book, few people will return it. I've used that line a lot, and no one has ever asked for a refund.

Sign: This is the fun part. Always ask the customer who they want it signed to and jot down the name on paper before you write it in the book. That way, you will not misspell their name. It doesn't matter how common the name is, it can have a different spelling. I had a Sue spelled S-i-o-u-x, and Mary spelled M-e-r-r-y, and a Jessica spelled with a Y instead of an I. My favorite was a man named Bob. Before I wrote his name, I asked, "B-o-b?" He looked at me very seriously and said, "No, you spelled it backwards."

Usually, while I'm signing the book, I hand the customer a card that has lines for their name and email address, then I ask for their information for my newsletter. You can also use a sheet of paper with designated headings. It doesn't matter what you use, but don't skip the step. At this point, I inform them that I'll let them know when I release new books. I also ask if they use Kindle or a Kindle app. If they answer in the affirmative, I explain how inexpensively they can buy the rest of the series as eBooks.

Tell: It's important to request that the reader tell their friends if they liked the book. You can ask them to write a review as well, but always give some instruction that will help build your readership. This may be your only opportunity to do that, especially if the new reader doesn't have an email account.

Book Clubs

One of my favorite places to sign is at private book clubs. They are usually small intimate groups so you don't need to be afraid of speaking and most of the members are thrilled to have you as a guest. Many, if not all, will have read your book and have positive things to say about it. Again, we're going on the assumption that you wrote a good book.

Book clubs can be hard to locate, but not difficult to set up for events once you find them. Most are looking for something different to do at their meetings, and what could be better than having an author speak? If there are ten or twelve people in the club, that's a dozen books you've already sold. If you have additional novels, you will often sell them at the meeting as well. Once these people know you, they are more likely to recommend your work to others.

How do you find book clubs? There are no lists on the internet. Or at least I haven't found any legitimate ones, because most are private groups that have no need to post online. You'll have to find them through your contacts. Whenever you do an event with the public and meet readers, ask if they belong to a book club. If they do, follow up a few days later and try to arrange something. You can chat with your friends online, and if you discover they have a book club (and are within your reach), you can send a private message asking if they are interested in having a speaker.

Book clubs do not need to be local, you can use Skype to attend their meeting. These are not generally as good as the in-person events, but better than not doing it at all.

One of my favorite book-club events was with a group called "Mostly We Eat Bookclub." They had an incredible food spread. Another was named "Read and Wine—Not for Whiners." Needless to say, they had some really good wine and laughed a lot.

Service Clubs & Other Community Organizations

Groups such as Kiwanis, Rotary, Soroptimist, Lions Club, and others are constantly looking for speakers. I've always made great book sales from these groups whenever I've given a presentation. Most are business people and they understand you are as well, so they're open to supporting your small enterprise.

Libraries

Libraries are a great place to gain public-speaking

experience. Often, the group will be very small. But if you need to practice speaking and talking about your book, this is a great place to do it. The people who show up will likely be very appreciative. Just don't expect to sell a lot of books at library events because the attendees are used to borrowing them from the library. There are a few exceptions to this rule. Some have a very active Friends of the Library group that will put on big events. I have been to a few with as many as a hundred attendees. Those are great events for selling books.

Whenever I do these events, big or small, I always give a copy of my book to the library. I also do library events for another reason. It's my way of paying back for all the wonderful hours I spent in libraries as a child. If it weren't for libraries, I may not know how to read. I certainly wouldn't have had the success or the adventures I've had without them. We only had two books in our home growing up. One was the Bible, and the other was a picture book my godmother gave me. I still have both. My older sisters would bring home books from the library, and one sister taught me how to read before I went to school. When I was a little older, I would bring home book after book from the local public library. I was thrilled with the knowledge I gained and the adventures I had through books.

Outside the Box

Don't limit yourself to the usual book signing places.

Take a close look at your genre and your subject matter and find other events that might match up. For instance, my books are about an attorney who practices law in juvenile court, so I've done several book signings and speaking events at CASA trainings. CASA, which stands for Court Appointed Special Advocates, is an organization that helps abused children in juvenile court.

I taught school for twelve years before I became an attorney, and subsequently an author. I have spoken at several teacher retirement groups and at some attorney organizations. You need to think outside the box and find what fits for you. It's not always about the subject matter of the book. It could be something that fits you, your character, your career, or your hobbies.

I have a colleague, Eric Peterson, who wrote a great novel called *The Dining Car*, told from the point of view of a former football star hired as a bartender aboard Horace Button's vintage private railroad car. Horace Button is a cantankerous, legendary food critic, and so the adventure begins. The author has done many events at wineries, restaurants, and train related organizations, because he thinks outside the box. (By the way, if you haven't had a chance to read Eric's book, it's worth checking out.)

I know of an author whose protagonist was a hairdresser. She traveled across the country doing meet-and-greets at beauty salons. Think about the professions and hobbies of your characters and use them to find your signing venues.

Another thing I discovered that works for me is signing at home-improvement shows and tradeshows. Home shows work better because you have a wider range of people there. The home shows are still not as good as book festivals because most attendees at book festivals are readers, but they are still well worth the effort. Not everyone who attends a home show is a reader, but some are, and no other authors are doing it, so I have no competition. Other events, such as craft shows or music and art festivals, can also be a good source and have less-expensive booth fees. The important thing to remember is that if there is a crowd, some of them are readers.

You should memorialize every event with photos that you can use later on your website or social media platforms. It is even better to post on Facebook or Twitter while you are at the event, which may even attract some locals.

Other Ways to Build Your Email List:

Some of you may have circumstances that don't allow you to get out and do events. If you live in a rural area where crowds don't gather or are homebound and can't get out, there are still things you can do. Meeting readers is the best way, because once they know you as a person, they are more likely to stick with you throughout your career. But it's not the *only* way. There are other means of keeping in touch, especially in this age of communication.

Use Your Book

Your book is a great source for building a list. Every book in every form—whether it be digital, paperback, or audio—should include a notice asking readers to email you. If so, you will receive a lot of emails from readers telling you what they thought of your book. Most of it will be very positive. Once in a while, you will receive an email from someone who found an error. That's even better, because now you can fix it. Either way, you can respond, add the reader to your email list, and start to get to know him or her. If the person cared enough to send you an email, you need to treat them with respect and communicate in return. It's important to tell the reader that you have added them to your list but that they can unsubscribe at any time.

There are other ways to use your book to obtain readers. One of the most effective I have found are Reader Magnets. By that I mean promotional campaigns that attract readers and their emails to you.

Pay for List-Building

Do NOT pay for an artificial list to build your own. You'll discover that it is not worth the time or money you put into it. In addition, you'll be paying extra for your email marketing service that you use to send your campaigns.

Do NOT use list-building groups that give away anything other than your book, or books very similar to yours. Doing so will give you a large but useless list. It's not about having a large list; it's about having a large audience.

What is available? One thing that works effectively is cross promoting with other authors in your genre. You can team up and promote for each other. You can do this in small groups and offer a book giveaway, then share the results with each other.

There are cross-promotion groups that do this very thing and are well worth the investment. These sites bring authors together from the same genre to conduct a giveaway. Each author gives away a free book and, in return, gets email addresses for people who read their genre. When you participate, the cost includes the price of the book you give away and the fee to the organizer. The price is usually minimal and well worth it.

Right now, there are two cross-promotional groups I use. I say 'right now' because book marketing changes so quickly that you need to keep up. Once you know what you're looking for, you can follow the forums for your genre and search for these things yourself. The two sites I've recently had great success with are: Authors Cross-Promotion, and BookSweeps.

Caveat: Do not do these promotions so often that your own readers get sick of them. Offer a free book only every six months. The people who sign up will be bombarded with emails, and if they get too much of that, you will lose them from your list.

Involve Your Readers

Once you have a list of readers, whether it's five or five thousand, you need to involve them in your work. I started doing it because it was fun, and I truly like getting to know my readers. Besides, I discovered early that they are a great source for many of the things we need to do as writers. That said, do not overload your readers with unnecessary emails. You need to find a good balance.

If there's something going on with your books, let readers know. That doesn't mean you need to send an email every week. When I have a new book coming out, my readers hear from me every week or so, but otherwise, I keep in touch at least every two months.

My readers help me with all sorts of things, from the book title to the launch. When I release a book, I ask my readers for suggestions for a new title. My first series has titles that follow the alphabetical order, so I ask for suggestions for the next letter. The F-word name-contest was fun. Sometimes I even get suggestions for a new plot. Although I haven't used one exactly as pitched, they often lead me to a new idea. Always respond to your emails when you get one.

My readers also choose my book cover. I have my book designer create three or four covers, then let readers select the one they like best. It has been interesting to note that they seldom choose the one I prefer. But I always go with their choice, because they know what they like.

I communicate with readers the most around the time I release a book, including the launch itself, which I'll talk about more in a later chapter. During my heavy writing time, I don't reach out as often. I will sometimes send an email campaign just to keep in touch, possibly for a holiday, or to let them know I haven't forgotten them and that something will be coming soon.

Communicate

I can't emphasize this enough. Always answer your emails. Always answer your social media posts. As long as you don't get bogged down reading all the extra stuff on your social media accounts, it takes only a few minutes every day to keep these current.

Reviews

Reviews are an important tool for writers. Many of the sites where you can advertise your books require ten or more reviews before you can place an ad. Some sites that do featured deals, such as BookBub, don't allow you to participate until you have a certain number of reviews. With your first book, it is more difficult to get reviews. You may need to call on friends and family and hope they will write an honest review for you.

Once you are established and have an email list, you can call on readers to review your books. I send them a copy (often an eBook) before the launch, then they can be prepared to write a review the day the book releases. If you do this, you will learn which readers to send copies to the second time around. That doesn't mean you rule out anyone who didn't give you a five-star review. If you have all five-star reviews, other readers will think they are all fixed or paid for. Although, the majority of my reviews are four and five stars, I get my share of others as well. The one-star reviews are hard to take, but not everyone will like everything you write. The four and five stars motivate me to keep writing.

If you put a notice in the back of your book asking for reviews, you will likely get more than you need to conduct the ad campaigns. There are also a lot of reviewers who write blogs and are more than willing to review your book. You just need to do your homework find them in your genre. My favorite for mystery writers is James Moushon, who is also a great mystery writer himself. He has a well-known blog called HBS Author's Spotlight where he regularly showcases authors and their books. He is a true champion of writers and does all he can to help promote books for others.

Blog Tours

There are many other book-review blogs available for online book tours or just to post a review. You can find them by starting with a Google search, then narrowing the list down to the ones who read your genre. After that, you need to find the contact for that blog and email them to ask if they would be interested. It's time consuming, but a great way to get exposure for your book.

Newsletter Campaigns

Now that you have an email list, what do you do with it? Use it to communicate with your audience in a professional, interesting manner. Newsletters can be done in numerous ways and in many different forms. Some writers send out a newsletter every month with something of interest to their readers. When I use the term *newsletter*, I'm referring to a mass email you send to your whole reader list. Therefore, I only send them when I have an announcement. That could be a new release of a paperback, eBook, or audiobook. Whenever I have a new novel coming out, I send newsletters about every three weeks, starting three/four months in advance. I let my readers vote on the book cover, then I reveal the book cover. I also announce the launch date, remind them of the launch, and announce promotions or giveaways. When the audiobook is ready, I let them know about that too. By the time I get through all that with one book, I'm starting on another and asking for input and sending notices to my list. If there is a lull, I sometimes send readers information about another writer who has a new release.

What goes into a newsletter? First, develop an image for the top of your newsletter, then use it consistently so recipients recognize where the email is coming from. Your image should include a photo of you and a tagline. Every few years, you should update the photo, but your tagline can be forever. My tagline is: *Author, Attorney, Advocate.* Develop something that fits both you and your writing.

Your subject line should be something that attracts attention. Keep in mind that for readers, something about a new book will likely be of interest. Here are a few examples: Book Cover Reveal, Facebook Launch of The Advocate's Illusion, Audiobook Now Available for Mason's Missing.

Your news or message should be brief and located

right after your image. Don't be afraid to also use other images, such as your book cover or photos of an event you attended. To the right of my message, I put my schedule or other book covers I have. One goes to the right, and the other is placed underneath my main message. I mix these up from time to time, but it's important to include both in every newsletter. Always attach a link to your cover image so readers can click it and land on a site where the book can be purchased. I link mine directly to Amazon.

After you compose a newsletter, always send yourself a test copy and check it over carefully. You don't want it going out with any errors. Make sure you check all the links to determine if they are working.

Give Back

It's important to give back, not only as an author, but as a community member. You will become a part of a vast writing community. Along the way, you'll encounter other writers who need your help. When you do, please assist them.

When your readers do things for you, such as writing reviews, don't forget to pay them back as well. There are many ways you can do this. One is to simply send a thank you note, which is very easy in this email age. You can also send copies of your book or swag or anything that shows you appreciate what they've done. You can acknowledge them in the front matter of your book. Another thing I often do is to use their names for characters. Sometimes I have a contest for the use of their name in the book.

Oh, and did I mention you need to communicate?

~ ~ ~

Step 2: Create an Audience—Bottom Line

Your list of readers is always a work in progress. There are numerous ways to develop your list, but the best is the in-person contacts you make. For the people you haven't met, you can build a good relationship through communication. Keep your list effective by purging the subscribers who never open your campaigns and by being kind to the ones who do.

Chapter 3

Step 3—Create a Marketing Plan

Another important step is to create a marketing plan to use as your guide. It will help you understand what to do next, keep the process moving, and stay within your budget.

Your marketing plan should consist of an outline, a calendar, daily tasks, a launch list, and a budget. The steps I have set up for you here can be the basis of your outline. You only have to add the details and specifics.

The Budget

The first thing you should determine is budget. If that is zero, then start with the things that don't cost any money. This will definitely limit you, so at some point, you need to find a way to add some marketing dollars to your efforts. Remember, this is a business, and it needs to be treated as such, whether you are traditionally published or independent.

If you have any money to spend on marketing, first decide what the amount is annually. Then break it down into monthly or weekly amounts. Some of the most-effective promotions can cost upward of $500 for a single ad. Therefore, if you have only $600 to spend for the year, it may be wise to use $500 on a single promotion that you know will be effective, rather than breaking it down to $50 a month. Those decisions depend on your resources, your genre, and what you decide to do in your marketing plan.

Market Every Day

It is important to do at least one thing every day that promotes your work. That may consist of Facebook posts, Twitter posts, a walk in the park where you hand out bookmarks, or talking about your books to the plumber who came to fix your pipes. It does not give you license to be obnoxious. There are subtle ways you can promote your books without being pushy.

One Signing a Month

You should try to set up one signing a month. Some of you may find it difficult to do one a year, but once you get used to the process, it will become easier. That does not necessarily mean just bookstores. More than likely, those signings will be at book festivals, craft festivals, the Rotary club, libraries, or other venues mentioned earlier. Many social-service organizations are constantly looking for speakers. Take advantage of what is near you. They don't cost you anything, and they are great opportunities to sell books, collect email addresses, and just get your name known.

If you have a budget that warrants it, or I should say, *when* you reach a budget that warrants it, do one paid promotion each month. Ads can range from five dollars to whatever you can afford. The main caveat is to not waste your money. There are many promotional spots that are just not worth anything. Unfortunately, you may have to test some. I have tried Facebook ads, Amazon ads, BookBub ads, and hundreds of small companies that claim to promote your books. The unfortunate thing about book advertising is that a lot of campaigns will work for a while, then they stop working. I believe part of the reason is that the email list they send their ads to doesn't grow fast enough to keep up with the numbers of promotions. After a while, the same people are receiving the ad over and over, but they either already bought your book or decided they didn't want it. If a campaign works at first, then stops working, just quit using it and move on. You have to keep a constant eye on the market and make adjustments.

Keep in mind that sometimes your ads may not generate sales but you are getting exposure. Some programs require you to pay a set amount for the number of impressions you receive, which includes everyone who sees your ad. In other circumstances, the cost is per click, which means you only pay if the reader actually clicks onto your ad. Those clicks don't necessarily translate to sales. You have to be vigilant in your watch of what you get from your ads. I find the per-click ads to be the most effective. I have spent hundreds of dollars and only gotten 10,000 impressions. But if you pay per click, you may get 10,000 impressions and only five click-throughs, which means you pay nothing for 9,995 of those impressions. Those kinds of ads are worth maintaining. You can run them on Amazon, BookBub, and Google, to name a few. But before you spend your hard-earned dollars on a paid ad, make sure you know exactly what you're getting.

Do NOT run ads or promotions that bombard your social media sites with sales pitches. Your friends will get annoyed, stop reading them, and possibly un-friend you. And those messages will not help sell books. Treat your social media friends as if they are your real-life friends.

Change Your Marketing Plan

This is a business, and your marketing plan is always a work in progress. You need to keep it updated, funded, and moving along.

~ ~ ~

Step 3: Create a Marketing Plan—Bottom Line

Right now is the time to start creating a marketing plan and developing a budget. Keep track of what you do, what works, and what doesn't. Don't be afraid to change your plan. Don't forget to do some marketing every day.

Chapter 4

Step 4—Create a Social Media Platform

In this age, you must have an online presence if you want to be a successful author. Unfortunately, just having that presence does not guarantee success. There are many social media sites online. You cannot do them all. You must choose the ones that work best for you and spend quality time on each. It is better to have one or two social media platforms that you actually have time for, than it is to have twenty that get little or no attention.

Successfully establishing an online presence is all about building relationships. Don't wait until your book is released, start now. It takes time to develop good relationships, but if you spend ten minutes a day, or an hour a week, building your friends by sharing things of interest, you'll soon have a decent following. If you have trouble thinking of things to post or tweet, simply share what others have said or done. Be careful though to not share something that isn't real, especially if it can be controversial.

Website

Having your own website is an absolute must. You need it for credibility. It will serve as your storefront and show people you actually exist. When I developed my first website, I set it up myself. It wasn't fancy, but it was clean and simple. I am not a computer whiz by any stretch of the imagination, but with a little research, I was able to set up my site. There are several online platforms that make it easy to create a website. I used WordPress, but a little online research will point you to many others. You also need to have your own URL/ website address. I purchased mine from GoDaddy, but you can google other sources and compare. You can also set up several and have them all funnel into your website.

What should you call your website? If your own name is available, that is the best way to identify your website. For example, my online address is www.teresaburrell.com. If you have a common name, that URL is likely not available, but you may be able to add *author* or *writer* to the end. For example, my friend's website address is www.jimstevenswriter.com. I don't recommend that you use the name of your book or the name of your series for your website— unless you plan to have a website for each series or book, which would not be good branding. If you have already purchased a URL with your book name, you can direct it to a website with your name.

If you cannot set up the website for yourself and don't have a young family member with technological abilities, then you can hire a professional. After a few years of working with my simple website, I hired a webmaster to design one for me. I use Chris Graham, whose email address is chrisg@bksp.org. Chris gives a break to authors. Another good web designer is Indy Quillen, who also happens to be an author. She can be found at www.indyquillen.com. Do your research and find what is affordable for you.

Social Media Platforms

As I stated earlier, there are many social media sites you can participate in, but some are more of a must-do than others. At a bare minimum, it is important to post on Facebook and Twitter. These two sites dominate the social media arena. If you can only handle two sites, these are the ones where you should be active.

Another good site for authors is Goodreads. Other sites you may want to consider are Pinterest, which has a visual focus, and Instagram, if your audience is a younger group such as millennials.

Facebook

Facebook is still the number one social media platform. The numbers are staggering. They include not only U.S., but worldwide interaction. More than two billion people log into Facebook on a monthly basis. That's a lot of potential readers and should be a big part of your marketing strategy, especially with baby boomers who still buy a lot of books.

I joined Facebook kicking and screaming, but my first publisher told me I needed to, so I did. It has since become a great platform for me. I have been able to connect with many people from my past and with many readers who otherwise I would not know. When you start Facebook, surround yourself with friends and family. Practice socializing with them. Talk to them online as you would in person. Once you get good at socializing on Facebook, add other people. You can look for old classmates, readers, and people with your interests. Then treat your new friends the same way you would your old friends and family. Meaning, don't bombard them with "Buy my book, buy my book, buy my book."

Create a Facebook Fan Page

It is important to set up a Facebook author page. That way you can keep your family separate from your readers if you choose to. The author page is where you'll post news about your books. If your author page consists primarily of readers, they will appreciate information about new releases, awards, or any other book-related news. It's also a place where you can interact with your readers on a regular basis. There, you can involve your readers in book-cover choices, title options, and character-name decisions, especially if you need something quickly. When I'm writing and I need a new character name, I find them in one of four ways: I use the names of family or friends; I look at my email list and pick one of my loyal readers; I go to my Facebook fan page and put out a quick post asking for suggestions; and when all else fails, I use a name-generator program. My preference is to use the name of a reader or a suggestion from a reader.

The Launch

You can do book launches in person at a local venue, which are a lot of fun, but they're also costly. If you've never done one, you may want to try it with your first book. But you can also use Facebook. It's a great platform for launching your work. Whenever I have a new book release, even if I set-up an in-person launch, I also launch it on Facebook. I create an event page and invite my friends. I ask them to ask their friends, which increases the numbers. It's a lot cheaper than doing a launch in person, and you can draw a much larger crowd. More important, your readers will appreciate the activity because they can participate even if they are in another country.

Now that you have a fan page, you can prepare for your Facebook launch. This is an important part of any book release. Make it fun, but don't make it too long. The first Facebook launch I did was from nine in the morning until nine at night, and I did it without any help. It was crazy, but it taught me a good lesson. Now, they last about four hours and I use a helper. Even so, they can be exhausting. You have to constantly create posts and keep it interesting so your attendees don't get bored. You also have to react to the posts from your audience. I hold contests and give out prizes, while my assistant watches the Comment Picker (or some other "pick a winner generator"). As people come onto the site, they are automatically entered into the drawings. When it comes time to pick a winner, my assistant hits select and the name is chosen. The first time I did a Facebook launch, I wrote out names and threw them in the hat. Using a generator is way easier. There are numerous programs with this capability available. Some are free, others charge monthly but offer other features besides this one. Woobox and ShortStack are two examples of good monthly programs.

Form a Street Team

What exactly is a street team? The closest I can come to a comparison is that it's equivalent to the old-style fan club people would form for a movie star. Although, a street team is more than that. The team actively works to help promote the author. I was approached by a reader who asked if she could set one up for me. At the time, I didn't know what it was. With a quick Google search, I soon discovered how much I needed one. If you have not reached the level where someone is approaching you, you can still set one up, and I recommend it highly. I expect that you'll discover some very loyal fans. Every author should have a street team.

How do you get a street team going? If you are just starting out, you may have to call on friends and/or family to participate. If you have a mailing list of readers, you can send a letter to your list, outlining what a street team does and asking if they're interested in participating. You may have to start with as few as four or five people, but if they are the right people, they'll help you a great deal.

Here is a sample letter to your readers.

Dear Reader,

Do you love reading mysteries? Delight in telling other people about the last book you read? Do you spend time online (social media, blogging)? Are you willing to pass out bookmarks to other mystery readers? Then you might be a perfect addition to my street team!

I have had so many inquiries from readers about my

street team, I decided to provide more information. However, I don't want to bother those who have no interest, so I'll send the next email regarding this subject only to those who answer Yes.

The purpose of the group is to help create buzz about my books and gain new readers for the series.

Incentives:

- You'll receive an autographed character card that only street team members have, as well as other swag.

- You get more personal interaction with the author.

- You get a sneak preview of book covers and plot points before the public does.

- You get to help pick character names. Whenever I need a name, I always ask the street team for suggestions first.

If you are interested, please click Yes. I'll send information, and you can decide if you want to join.

Sincerely,

Teresa

Make sure you have some kind of Yes/No button at the bottom of your letter. Most email marketing services will have one you can insert. When you receive the responses, you only need to answer the Yes comments, unless you get questions from others who are undecided. Remember, this is an initial quest for interest, and not all of these readers will want to be a member. Some are just seeking information at this stage.

Your next step is to send an email outlining what is expected of team members. Make it clear that they do not need to do everything on the list. Many will do a lot of the suggestions, but most will only participate in a few. That's okay. Everything they do for you brings attention and exposure to your books.

Make sure you have your group page set up on Facebook before you invite members. The street team page is different from your fan page because it's private and invitational only. The group page doesn't have to be complete with images, a name, etc. Let the members help you with the particulars. Once you have invited your readers, give them specific instructions on how to join. I usually send an email with the URL so they can just click and get to my street team page. On the landing page, they need to click the Join button, then one of the admins will accept them. I ask them to email me their postal mailing address so I can send a token of my appreciation. I have developed special cards for three of my characters. I have printed a hundred cards of each character and given them to only the most loyal readers. I mail the members an autographed collector card and a thank-you note for joining, but you can show your appreciation however you choose.

If you have readers who are interested in joining but are not on Facebook, do not leave them out. As long as they use email, you can communicate with them. I have a small group on my street team who are great participants, but are not on Facebook.

When setting up your Facebook group page, the first order of business is to let your team pick their own name. After all, it's their group. Someone needs to put a simple graphic at the top of the page that depicts the team. It's important that you keep the group closed, except by invitation. These are your most loyal fans, and you need to give them the respect they are due. They should be the first to hear any news about your books. My street team is the first to know when I have a new release, the first to know when I have a big promotion, and the first to help me choose a book cover. In short, before I send an email campaign to my readers list, I always inform my street team of the news first. Some of them will receive copies of the book before it is released so they are ready with reviews on launch day.

What does your street team do for you? Their participation is only limited by your imagination or theirs. I often get beta readers from this group. Many of my street team members will write book reviews on Amazon, Goodreads, Barnes & Noble, and other sites. For members who want them, I send bookmarks to pass out in their hometowns. Those who are on Goodreads are quick to mark my books *To Read*. Those who are on BookBub follow me. They also follow me on Amazon, which seems to help with those algorithms. I have been invited to speak at book clubs and other events through my street team. They talk about my books on social media sites and promote my hashtag #TheAdvocateSeries.

Some members ask their local library to order the book, or they donate a copy themselves. They also do this at their church libraries or community centers. If they are part of a service club, they tell the group about the book and often ask me to speak. They suggest my novel to their book clubs and also direct readers to my website. Some members have bought my books as Christmas or birthday gifts. They pin the cover to Pinterest and share their favorite quotes from the book online. If they purchase the eBook on Kindle, they can highlight their favorite lines, which gives Amazon viewers something to chatter about. Some members will host a speaking event, but most will simply like my posts, share my links, and re-tweet my tweets. Still, the list is endless.

What can you do for your street team? As I said before, you need to treat your social media contacts as you would your in-person friends. They are not just names or photographs; they are people. Be kind, be courteous, and be thoughtful. When someone does something for you, at the very least you need to thank them. There are other ways, however, to show your street team they are appreciated. When you have a new member join the team, follow the same steps you did when you first formed the team: ask for their mailing address and send them a thank-you letter.

When I have a new book coming out, I ask my designer to create four or five covers. My street team looks at them and votes on their favorite, narrowing it to three covers. Then I send those images to my entire reader list and take another vote to determine which cover I will use. My street team always gets the first look though.

When I need a name for a character I will post in the group and ask for suggestions. Often times, I will use the name of one of my street team members. There are many ways you can thank your team for what they do to help you.

Twitter

This is another important site where you can engage with an audience. I know authors who have built a large reader base through Twitter. I have not done that personally. I find it more difficult than Facebook, but I've been told once you master it, the platform can be very beneficial. I'm still on the learning curve. The one thing I can say with certainty is that the rules are the same for every site—treat people as you would treat them in person. Do not try to sell your books. Provide information and interact with people. There is a reason it is called *social* media.

Social media sites are also a good place to network with other writers in your genre. Get to know your fellow authors and develop relationships. Perhaps some cross promotion will be in your future.

Author Organizations

If you are a mystery, suspense, or crime writer, joining International Thriller Writers is an absolute must. Not only does the organization offer ways to grow your readership, it is also a great way to network with other authors in your genre and to keep in touch with what's going on in the crime fiction area. Mystery Writers of America is another group you can join if you're traditionally published. Crime Writers have several big conferences good for networking. There is Left Coast Crime, ThrillerFest, and Bouchercon to name a few.

Most other genres have networking groups as well. Romance writers have several writing organizations and conferences. One of the biggest is Romance Writers of America Conference. Sci-fi and fantasy have SFWA Nebula Conference and others. Fantasy has World Fantasy Convention, which has been running since 1975. The horror genre has StokerCon. Whatever your genre, find your groups and get involved.

Amazon

Amazon is a great source for building your readership. Whether you use the retailer exclusively or not depends on you. Either way, don't discount the importance of Amazon. You must set up a profile and author page on Amazon.com. Use Author Central and fill in every blank space you can on your author page.

Goodreads

Goodreads is another must, even though it's not the easiest site to maneuver through. If you're not familiar with Goodreads, I suggest you watch any tutorials you can find and spend a little time getting to know the site. It attracts a lot of readers and like any other social media site, you need to interact with other members for it to be effective.

Blogs

There was a time when blogging was a great way to build a reading audience, but the internet has been flooded with blogs, and the platform has lost some of its appeal. Should you have a blog? If it takes away time from something else that's more productive, then I say no, or at least to limit your time. If, however, you already have a blog following or if you have something that directly relates to your book that may attract a large audience, then I say go for it. Even if you don't have your own blog, you can do interviews, write guest posts, and get reviewed on other established sites. Blog tours can be very effective if you do your homework and connect with active sites.

BookBub

This is an important promotional platform in the book world. BookBub is one of the few remaining ways to advertise and connect with a very large audience. At the very least, you should sign on as an author and develop a following on the site. If you can get your book accepted for a Featured Deal, their newsletter can give your sales a boost. BookBub ad spaces are now available to purchase as well. But whether or not you spend money on this site, you need to establish a profile there.

~ ~ ~

Step 4: Social Media—Bottom Line

You can't do it all, so pick and choose wisely where you spend your time. Build relationships and they will come.

Chapter 5

Step 5—Pay for Ads & Other Promotional Sources

I suggested earlier that part of your marketing plan should include paid ads. Again, I caution you to be careful how you go about this. One thing you should do is to keep in touch with the many chat forums and blogs in your genre and see what other authors say is currently working. This market changes quickly, and the only way to keep up is by staying involved and watching what is going on. As of this writing, I can only tell you what works for me. At the top of that list is still BookBub, although it does not have the same impact it had a couple of years ago.

BookBub Ads

BookBub offers a program called the Featured Deal. To get one of these promotional spots, you have to apply and request a date (or a range of dates). Before you pay for this service, which can cost up to a thousand dollars, BookBub reviews your request and lets you know whether you were accepted. The cost depends on several factors: the genre you choose, the discounted sale price you set for your book, and which countries you want to reach. Some of their genre categories have more than 3 million followers, but you can easily pay more than $500 to reach that many people. Is it worth it? Historically, it has absolutely been worth it. I have always garnered a positive return on my investment. Usually, that happens the first day, but you also get residuals for several days or weeks.

Why not do BookBub every week? The answer is simple. Because you can't. BookBub limits any given book to a featured deal once every six months. It limits the author to once every thirty days. It also restricts how often you can apply if you have been turned down. But more important, BookBub receives thousands of submissions every month, and they only include five to ten books in their newsletter each day. Therefore, it has become more and more difficult to get a featured deal.

BookBub now includes ads you can purchase on a cost-per-impression basis. As of this writing, they also have a cost-per-click program in beta testing. As I stated earlier, I've found cost-per-click ads to be effective for getting exposure for minimal money, even if you don't make immediate sales.

Facebook Ads

There is a real art to writing Facebook ads. The process can be confusing, and you can waste a lot of money trying to become effective. I suggest that if you plan to run Facebook ads, contact the company and let them explain the process. There are also good YouTube videos that can be helpful. I know some writers who have had great success with Facebook ads. Just be careful because the cost can add up quickly.

Amazon Ads

I spoke briefly about Amazon ads before, and I suggest again that you choose the cost-per-click process. Before you run these ads, you need to get a good understanding of how they work. I do not have the expertise to explain that here. However, there are many good books written on the subject.

There are also some ads (not necessarily through Amazon) that will help build your Amazon following, which is a great idea because it helps to trigger the Amazon algorithms which encourages Amazon to advertise for you. One thing to keep in mind is that Amazon does not reveal how many followers you actually have, so there is no way of knowing whether some of your ads are working.

Many small companies claim to advertise your book, and they charge dearly for it. What I have discovered is that some programs work for a short period, then they are no longer effective at selling books. I suggest that if you try some of these, keep good records. If you are not seeing increased sales, move on.

Free Ads

Yes, there are some free ads available, especially when you put your book online for free. If you conduct a giveaway, you might as well use every free site available to advertise for you. There is a list of some of the sites I have used in the past. You need to check these out carefully because they can change quickly and some of them work for a while and then they seem to stop. However, using these free sites can give you a lot of exposure for little or no cost.

Conferences & Genre Organizations

Most genre fiction has at least one organization that supports its writers, such as Sisters in Crime, Romance Writers of America, or Science Fiction Writers of America. Many of the organizations are national but have local chapters. Find your organization, join it, and participate in any way you can. The more involved you are, the more you will gain from the experience.

Writers have access to two different kinds of conferences: those tailored strictly to writers, and those geared to both authors and readers. If you need to hone your writing skills or learn about marketing, you should attend writers' conferences. I always come away from them motivated to sit down and write, amazed at what I have learned in a few short days. One that I have found to be extremely beneficial is Southern California Writers' Conference. It was the first writers' conference I ever attended, and it was invaluable. I went back the next few years and learned a great deal about writing. Then I submitted twenty pages to a publisher for an advanced read, and she asked for my manuscript. That's how I landed my first publisher. I now often teach marketing classes at the Southern California Writers' Conference in San Diego and in Irvine, California.

Conventions where writers mix with readers are also very worthwhile. Most are genre specific. Because I write mysteries, I've attended Left Coast Crime, Bouchercon, Writers' Police Academy, and Thrillerfest. I make an effort to attend at least one or two conventions a year where I can network with other authors and meet readers. The knowledge you gain from these events are well worth the cost. Whatever your genre, you can usually find a reader convention that fits. Romance writers have many to choose from, with the most popular being Romance Writers of America. Fantasy and sci-fi writers have several conventions as well, such as Comic-Con, ReaderCon, and Science Fiction Writers of America Conference.

If you do an internet search for these organizations, you'll likely find something in your vicinity that you can attend. There are many conferences and conventions in other countries too.

Publicists

Let me start by saying there are some excellent publicists available. It is difficult, however, to find one who really knows how to market in this crazy, fast-paced book industry. I have spent thousands on publicists, and unfortunately most of their efforts did not work for me. One thing I did wrong was to hire a publicist before I was ready. I had not developed a strong platform or a marketing plan. I had done my job—I wrote the book. Wasn't it the publicist's job to take it from there? Wrong. There's more to it than that. If you want information about how to get ready for a publicist, or if you are debating whether to hire one, there are many books that cover the subject. One I would recommend is *The Tao of Book Publicity* by Paula Margulies.

Publicists can be an important part of your marketing plan. If done correctly with the right person, publicity can be a positive, worthwhile experience. Always get references from the publicist. It is also extremely important to get a referral from an author who has had success before spending your money. Publicists are not cheap, but if they are good at their job, the cost would certainly be worth it.

One thing you can do when you speak to a publicist is to ask for references. Then follow up with them. If someone gives you a reference to tout their work, it will likely be an author who has something positive to say about them, but that is not always the case. Sometimes when you question these writers, you will discover what makes the publicist worthwhile. Always look to see what kind of standing those authors have in the bookselling world. To my chagrin, most of the author references I have received have book ratings far below mine. The ratings are fairly easy to see on Amazon. Each book is given a rating based on its reviews ranking from zero to five-stars. There is an Amazon Best Sellers Rank on each book, as well as an Author Rank for each author. When a publicist gives you a reference for an author he or she has worked with, check out their ranking and ratings. I realize there can be many factors for ratings, but if the publicist has been working for these authors and they cannot do better than I do on my own, why would I pay the publicist to promote me?

In theory, using a publicist is a great idea if you can afford it. He or she can help you launch a new release, they can get you speaking events, blog tours, radio and television spots, depending on your needs. So if you find a good publicist, it can be well worth the expense. As with anything else that you plan to spend your marketing dollars on, do your research.

Social Media Assistants

These specialists are exactly what the name says—someone who assists you with social media. This is an area that may be well worth budgeting for to help grow your online presence. If you are not comfortable on social media sites, an assistant could be particularly important. That doesn't mean you can just hand over the reins to someone else and never post a word yourself. You still need to stay involved. It is still your voice readers need to hear, but social media assistants can certainly help you maneuver through the system.

I personally like to answer all my own emails, but there are times when you can use an assistant to do this. You still need to draft the email, but if the task is to send the same message over and over again, your assistant can likely handle it for you.

~ ~ ~

Step 5: Paid Ads & Other Sources—Bottom Line

There are many advertising platforms in the book-selling market where you can waste your money. You will need to test the ads to find what works for you. Network with other writers, either at conferences or online, and find out what they think has been effective. If you can afford it, a publicist and/or social media assistant might be a good fit for you as well. Do your homework to find the best person you can for the price.

Join a local and/or national organization in your genre, and if you can, attend a conference once a year.

Chapter 6

Step 6—Create Marketing Materials

You can skip your morning latte and spend five dollars a day on marketing, or you can get a second mortgage on your house and invest thousands. I wouldn't encourage you to do the latter, but either way, I suggest that you make sure marketing materials are a part of your budget. These materials can range from inexpensive bookmarks to giving away a free cruise. Okay, the free cruise is a little extreme, but you get the point. There is no limit to what you can do, except for the cost.

Awards

Is it worth the time and energy it takes to submit your book to a writing contest? The first thing you need to know is that all awards are not alike. Some are worth a lot more than others. The Pulitzer Prize will get you a lot further than your local library Best Fiction Award will. Even though most of us will not be a Pulitzer Prize winner, that doesn't mean you can't get recognition from other nationally known honors.

There are many groups that provide awards for well-written books. Some are exclusive to self-published work or small-press books, so new authors don't have to compete with the big-name authors. I think I'm the proudest of my Best Mystery for San Diego award. We have many excellent writers in this city, and yet I was recognized for my book, THE ADVOCATE'S FELONY.

Several of my novels have received a Readers' Favorite Award, a respected international book contest. I have received three silver medals and one bronze, and this year I got my first gold.

If you keep submitting your books to different associations and you can't seem to even make the finalist list, then investing in writing contests may not be a good use of your money. However, if you do receive some recognition, you can list yourself as *an award-winning* author. Just make sure the contest you enter is legitimate. There are a lot of scams online. It is important that the writing world recognizes the award.

Posters/Signs

Posters or signs are a must for in-person events. The

sign should have the front cover of the book you are promoting, and I suggest the words *Author Book Signing* at the top. This provides enough information to get the attention of most people who would be interested.

Your poster needs to stand alone or at the very least on an easel. It should have a foam core, so it's both lightweight and stiff. Roll-up posters without a stand are difficult to work with because you often will not have a background to put them on. I prefer the retractable canvas banner that comes with its own stand. They roll up and go into a carrying case so they can be easily transported from one event to another.

Swag

Swag refers to the physical materials you use to promote your book. The most important are bookmarks. You *must* have bookmarks if you plan to sell paperback books or do in-person events. You must have a physical card to give to people when you speak to them. A bookmark needs a short description of your book and all your contact information. Do not put your phone number on the bookmark; use your business card for that. Your bookmark should include your email address, website address, and Facebook and/or Twitter addresses. It should also be colorful and attractive to the eye.

I keep a lot of swag on hand because I make personal

appearances all the time. I also use it for gifts for my book launches. I wrote earlier about my *collector cards* or *character cards*, as I call them, which I have had printed. My private investigator, JP, is a reader favorite so I had someone pose for a photograph. I only use his backside image because I don't want to reveal a face. I want my readers to identify with, and put their own image on my character. The card is set up like a baseball trading card. It's the same size and design as a trading card with a photo on the front and statistics on the back. You can use details such as height, birthplace, hometown, occupation, talents, or whatever is unique to your character. JP makes a lot of slang comments, and his friends call them JPisms. On the bottom of my card is always one of his JPisms.

Picking a model for the image can be risky because it will implant an image of your character in the minds of those who see the card. Make certain you find a model who you can use again later if you want to do another card. You can also use an image you buy online at places like Dreamstime or Shutterstock. If you do, I suggest you buy several different poses in case you need them in the future. They won't necessarily be available the next time you want to create a card.

Other swag items I give away are earrings that feature my books. My readers are always anxious to win a pair of these during a book launch. My sister makes the earrings for me, and they are unique. I suggest you consider your story and come up with something that fits your character that you can make or have made. For instance, my protagonist, Sabre, wears Jerry Garcia ties, so I occasionally sign one and give it away in a contest. Your readers will love it if you create something that embraces their favorite character.

I have tried many kinds of swag, some with more success than others. You have to see what works best for you. I often have pens with my name and email address on them. Pens are cheaper than other items you can have produced, but you're limited to what you can put on them. Hand sanitizer is nice, and you can buy the little plastic bottles with an image of your book cover on the front. But you'll have to hand them out, because the liquid is harder to mail. Microfiber cloths are always a big hit, and they're cheap to mail if you need to send them. I have ordered 6x6-inch microfiber cloths with all my books on them and others featuring just one book. They make a great visual, but you have to buy a large quantity (a minimum of 100) to get a decent price.

My character JP is a cowboy and since I spend a lot of time signing books in Southern California, Arizona, and Nevada, I had a fan made up in the shape of a cowboy hat that is particularly well-received by readers in the summer months. The fan also has a JPism on it.

Mouse pads are great gifts for launch parties, but they are too expensive to give out as swag. They look beautiful with your book cover printed across the front. Coffee mugs and pillows with your cover on them are also good launch gifts.

I have also used keychains, coasters, water bottles, T-shirts, and more. The list is endless. You are limited only by your bank account and your imagination, but the more relatable the item is to your books, the better.

~ ~ ~

Step 6: Marketing Materials—Bottom Line

Spend your marketing dollars on bookmarks, posters for signings, awards, and other swag. Do them in that order if you can. It's easy to go overboard on swag, so make sure it is something you need, not just something that's fun to have.

Chapter 7

Step 7—Give Books Away

Writers have strong, but contradictory, points of view about giving away books. One group claims that you should never give away your written word because it cheapens you and the industry. They claim that if you give away your product, you devalue it. I understand where they're coming from, but I disagree. If you give readers a short story or the first book in a series, they might want to read everything else you've ever written. Of course, this only works if your writing is good enough to leave readers wanting more.

Personally, I tend to subscribe to the *Mrs. Fields Original Cookie* marketing plan. Mrs. Fields gave away millions of cookies to build up her following. The Fields

Corporation owns TCBY, a yogurt distributor that also gives out samples—of yogurt, not cookies. I don't know if TCBY was the first to give out yogurt samples, but most yogurt stores do it now. The point is that it has proven to be an effective way to market, to get people interested in your product, and to encourage them to buy the rest of what you produce.

I'm sure you'll encounter naysayers when it comes to giving away a sample of your writing. I'm here to tell you that it has been a very effective way to build my readership. That said, if you only have one book and you give it away, you have nothing to sell. I now have ten books in my first series, and I am very confident that if someone reads the first book they will want to buy the rest.

Write a Short Story or Novella

What do you give away if you are just starting out? One thing you can offer is a chapter or two or five—whatever it takes to showcase your writing style and wet readers' appetite. One example of what I've done is to write a short story about one of my characters who had become a reader favorite. I use the short story on my website as a freebie for anyone who signs up for my email list. That does two things: 1) It helps build my email list, and 2) It introduces my writing to a new reader who will hopefully buy my books.

At book events, I always let people know I will send

them a short story if they sign up for my email list. When I get back to my office, I send a note to everyone whose email I collected, and I include a copy of the short story. I don't sell my short story to anyone. I use it only for marketing purposes. I can honestly tell people that it's not for sale because it's something special only for my readers.

Kindle Select

If you are not familiar with Kindle Select, I suggest you learn whatever you can about it. I'm not saying you should run out and sign up, but you should have a close look at what it offers. If you join Kindle Select, your eBooks will be exclusive to Amazon for a minimum of three months. There are two schools of thought regarding exclusivity to Amazon versus placing your work throughout the wide range of available distributors. On the surface, the choice seems easy. Why would you limit where you can sell your eBook?

It's not that simple. If you go with Kindle Select and become exclusive to Amazon, you will benefit from the advantages of the program. When you are exclusive to Amazon, you can participate in their subscription service, Kindle Unlimited (KU). KU gives its members access to millions of eBooks, which they can *borrow* from Kindle. There is no time limit as to how long they can keep them, but readers are restricted to ten books in their library at any one time. The advantage to authors is they are paid for these downloads. However, you don't get paid until the book is read, and the payment is per page. I have found the program to be quite lucrative. I generally earn at least three times as much in KU royalties than I do in actual book sales.

The disadvantage is that you must be exclusive to Amazon with your digital book. That means you cannot list your work in other eBook-reader platforms such as the Nook (Barnes & Noble) or Kobo. You can, however, sell it anywhere in paperback.

You have to make the decision about whether this works for you. I have tried both ways, and I always come back to Amazon. Maybe that's short sighted because the book-selling market is constantly changing. Perhaps tomorrow it will quit being profitable, but for now, that's what works best for me.

Kindle Select also allows you to give away your books for free for five days every three months. I find that to be effective as a marketing tool, sometimes in combination with a BookBub Featured Deal and sometimes on my own.

Paperback Print Run

Another thing you can do is contract with an independent printer to produce a large quantity of paperbacks. Let me start by saying that this is a big undertaking. It can cost thousands of dollars, but it has also proven to be worthwhile for me. You don't want to lead with this tactic. You must have other books for readers to buy to make this a good marketing strategy, and you must spend hours of time doing in-person events where you can sell or give away the copies.

If you decide to produce a large quantity, don't buy the paperbacks from a print-on-demand (POD) company. You must find a quality offset printer to do the run. Each book will likely cost about half of what you would pay Amazon, Ingram Sparks, or any POD printer. A few companies do both POD and offset print runs. If you produce your book with one of them, a print run will be easy. The problem is, to get the lower per-book cost, you have to order a minimum of about 2000 copies. For many authors, it would take a lifetime to sell or even give away that many books.

Why do a print run? If you are selling a lot of paperbacks in venues other than bookstores or online, then it might make sense just from a cost point. Or if you do numerous in-person events and have a series of books, you may want to use the first book as your *Mrs. Fields Cookie* sample. Last year, I paid a printer to produce 2000 copies of the first novel in my Advocate series. I average about one public appearance a month in which I give away 50 to 100 copies of that book. Sometimes, people would rather have the Kindle version. In that case, I make sure I obtain the email address they use on Amazon. When I get home, I gift them a copy of the first book in the series. Amazon sends the eBook directly to them. However, most readers standing in front of you will be thrilled to get an autographed copy of your book, then tell their friends and family about their newfound author.

I repeat, this *only* works if you have a series of books and the first book is good enough to entice them to read the rest.

Goodreads

Goodreads has an author program that allows you to give away as many eBooks or print copies as you choose. Readers enrolled in the site can sign up for a chance to win a copy of your book. The hope is that they will review it if they do. This process also gets a bunch of readers to mark your book *To Read* on the Goodreads site, which in turn gives you more exposure.

After the contest, Goodreads sends you the names of winners and their contact information so you can send them the books. They don't provide the names or email addresses of the people who sign up for the contest—only the winners. They also specify that you cannot contact the winners except to send the book. Goodreads is a well-respected site for readers and therefore is worth the effort. The cost can be minimal too. This is especially true of eBooks because there is no expense to send them. But even with paperbacks, if you only give away a few and limit the contest to US entries (to avoid expensive mailing costs), you can get a great deal of exposure for a small investment.

Genre Sites for Giveaways

You'll need to do some research to find the genre-specific sites that apply to your books. Many of these will let you conduct giveaways that may be worthwhile. For mystery authors, one site I suggest is International Thriller Writers. They have a monthly giveaway in which you can participate. Find the sites that apply to your work.

Charities

I am a sucker for charities, especially causes dealing with children. I have given away many baskets of books to be added to silent auctions or drawings. I do this as a way to pay back for the success I have had in my life. I imagine this probably improves my sales as well, but that isn't why I do it. Sometimes, you just do things because you can.

~ ~ ~

Step 7: Giveaways—Bottom Line

Giving readers a sample of my work has been a substantial part of the reason for my success. For this kind of marketing to work, you need to have a well-written book that makes the reader want more. You need to look to the future, not the immediate sale, and you must keep writing.

Chapter 8

Step 8—Write Another Good Book

I said in the beginning that the title of this book was originally *$0 to Six Figures in Seven Not-So-Easy Steps,* but in reality, there are *eight* steps. The next step is to write another good book. I did not say *another* book, I said another *good* book. Hopefully, it will be even better than the first one. You have to keep the books coming. Unless, you wrote the Great American Novel and got really lucky, you'll need more than one book to make a living.

You not only need more than one, but your next novel should be in the same genre. Each time you write a book in a new genre, you start over. Even better, write another story in the same series. That does not mean you can't be successful writing standalones. You can, but the marketing is more difficult.

I want to end with a reminder that one of the most important things you need to do as an author is to be kind to your readers. Treat them as you would like to be treated yourself. You'll probably have some strange, perhaps even bizarre, experiences on this writing adventure, but remember—without readers, you are just a writer. With readers, you can be a successful author.

Marketing Plan Guide

I.   Write a Book
- a. Set a date for completion of first draft
- b. Set time for editing
- c. Front and back matter for book
- d. Beta reading
- e. Cover design
- f. Book formatting
- g. Paperback
- h. Digital
- i. Set a date for launch
- j. Reviewers
- k. Audio

II.   Create an Audience
- a. Set up email marketing service
- b. Events to build list
  - i. Book festivals
  - ii. Book clubs
  - iii. Libraries
  - iv. Other book signing events
- c. Cross promotion

III.   Develop Your Marketing Plan
- a. Outline
- b. Calendar
- c. Daily list
- d. Launch list

IV. Social Media
   a. Website
   b. Facebook
      i. Fan page
      ii. Street team
   c. Twitter
   d. Amazon
   e. Goodreads
   f. Blogs
   g. BookBub

V. Paid Ads & Other Sources
   a. BookBub
   b. Facebook
   c. Amazon
   d. Others
   e. Free ads
   f. Publicists
   g. Social media assistant

VI. Marketing Materials
   a. Awards
   b. Swag
      i. Bookmarks
      ii. Mugs
      iii. Pens
      iv. Hand sanitizer
      v. Mouse pads
      vi. Pillows
      vii. Keychains

viii. Coasters

ix. Fans

VII. Giveaways
   a. Short story
   b. Kindle Select
   c. Print run
   d. Goodreads
   e. Genre sites
   f. Charities

VIII. Write Another Book

Launch List Timeline

6 Months Before Release

1. Start to research for subject matter sites on FB, Twitter, etc. (everyday)
2. Make contact and start to communicate

3 Months

1. Continue to communicate with subject-matter sites
2. Find cover designer and/or look for cover images

2 Months

1. Set release date
2. Set up pre-order on Kindle
3. Send campaign about pre-orders

4. Post cover choices to street team (narrow down to 2 or 3)

    a. One week later, send email campaign to all readers for a vote on cover

    b. Post the cover to your street team site

    c. Send campaign with the cover to your readers

5. Communicate with subject-matter sites (ongoing)

7 Weeks

1. Contact beta readers to see if they are still interested in reading

2. Send manuscript to beta readers (make sure they use tracking/Word doc)

6 Weeks

1. Newsletter with name of book and cover reveal

2. Tweet, Facebook posts, and Pinterest with cover reveal

3. Engage street team

4. Order bookmarks (www.gotprint.com)

5 Weeks

1. Plan activities for launch (giveaways, questions, games)

2. Upload book to Kindle for pre-order

3. Correct errors from beta readers

4. Format print and eBooks

5. Order paperback proof

4 Weeks

1. Newsletter with release date and launch notice

2. Tweet, Pinterest, and FB about release

3. Continue to communicate with subject-matter sites

4. Start to set up promotions (BookBub, etc.)

5. Set your first book for free on release date

6. Send invite for launch

7. Apply for Library of Congress number

8. Order paperbacks

9. Order promotional materials for launch

    a. Chapstick

    b. Collector cards (www.gotprint.com)

    c. Microfiber cloths

    d. Earrings

    e. Buttons www.purebuttons.com)

    f. Mugs (www.vistaprint.com)

    g. T-shirts

    h. Aprons

    i. Key chains (www.purebuttons.com)

    j. Coasters (www.purebuttons.com)

    k. Pens (www.penfactory.com)

    l. Canvas bag (www.vistaprint.com)

    m. Mouse pads (www.vistaprint.com)

3 Weeks

1. Ask beta readers to review book on Amazon/Goodreads/BookBub etc.

2. Contact other reviewers to see if interested in book
3. Send copies to reviewers
4. Set up BookBub for the first book in the series

2 Weeks

1. Newsletter with launch reminder
2. Set up Goodreads giveaway (3 print books of new release)

1 Week

1. Send reminder of launch
2. Make sure all promotions are in place for freebie

Launch Day

1. Morning, send launch reminder
2. Release book on KDP
3. Release book on Amazon

4. Be prepared with lists, etc.

5. Launch!

Post Launch

1. Send paperbacks to beta readers as a thank you

2. Send paperbacks to those reviewers who don't use digital

3. Fill orders for paperbacks

4. Update Amazon Page and Author Central with new book—all countries

5. Update any other sites that have your books listed

6. Set up BookBub for another book (six weeks after launch)

7. Keep track of reviews

8. Send book to Library of Congress

   Library of Congress
   US Programs, Law, and Literature Division
   Cataloging in Publication Program
   101 Independence Avenue, S.E.
   Washington, DC 20540-4283

9. ITW

10. Goodreads

11. Hire narrator for audiobook

12. When audiobook is done

      a. Post on ITW

      b. Post on Facebook, Pinterest, Twitter, etc.

      c. Put notice on Facebook at Free Audible

        Audiobook Giveaways

13. Write another good book

Websites

Conferences & Organizations

Bouchercon: www.bouchercon.com

ComicCon: www.comicon.com

Left Coast Crime: www.leftcoastcrime.org

Romance Writers of America: www.rwa.com

Sisters in Crime: www.sistersincrime.org

Southern California Writers' Conference: www.writersconference.com

Cross Promotion

Authors Cross-Promotion: www.authorsxp.com

BookSweeps: www.booksweeps.com

Marketing Websites

Choosy Bookworm: www.choosybookworm.com

Digital book Today: www.digitalbooktoday.com

eBook Daily Deals: http://author.ebookdaily.com/

ebook Discovery: www.ebookdiscovery.com

eBooks Habit: http://ebookshabit.com/for-authors/

eReader Café: https://theereadercafe.com/promote-your-books/

Free99Books: http://free99books.com/author/add

Freebooksy: https://www.freebooksy.com/for-the-authors/

Mega Book Deals: https://megabookdeals.com/for-authors/

NFKB: http://newfreekindlebooks.com/authors/

People Reads: http://www.peoplereads.com/list-your-ebook.html

Publicists

Paula Margulies: www.paulamargulies.com

Stock Photos

Dreamstime: www.dreamstime.com

Shutterstock: www.shutterstock.com

Swag Sites

GotPrint: www.gotprint.com

Pen factory: www.penfactory.com

Pure Buttons: www.purebuttons.com

Vista Print: www.vistaprint.com

Webmasters

Chris Graham: chrisg@bksp.org

Indy Quillen: www.indyquillen.com

Other Sites Mentioned

Acorn Publishing: www.acrornpublishingllc.com

Author Central: www.authorcentral.com

Bookbub: www.bookbub.com

Go Daddy: www.GoDaddy.com

Goodreads: www.goodreads.com

James Moushon:
http://www.hbsauthorspotlight.blogspot.com

Shortstack: www.shortstack.com/

Woobox: www.Woobox.com

Word Press: https://wordpress.com

ABOUT THE AUTHOR

Teresa Burrell has had several successful careers. She has taught school, practiced law, developed and ran her own business, and became a very successful author. Her education and many careers have given her the experience she needed to write her novels and the wherewithal to market them.

Her award-winning Advocate Series consists of ten novels so far and continues to grow. Teresa has also written *Mason's Missing*, the first book in The Tuper Mysteries Series, as well as three children's books.

She built her novel writing business into a six-figure annual income, teaches marketing at conferences, and has now written *$0 to Six Figures* so others can share her expertise. Her novels have received many awards and have all hit the best sellers' list on Amazon. Most have stayed there for months, and five of them were in the top 40 in the legal suspense category for well over a year.

Teresa is available for speaking events and seminars and is willing to travel. If you're interested, please contact her at Teresa@teresaburrell.com .

OTHER BOOKS BY TERESA BURRELL

THE ADVOCATE SERIES

THE ADVOCATE (Book 1)

THE ADVOCATE'S BETRAYAL (Book 2)

THE ADVOCATE'S CONVICTION (Book 3)

THE ADVOCATE'S DILEMMA (Book 4)

THE ADVOCATE'S EX PARTE (Book5)

THE ADVOCATE'S FELONY (Book 6)

THE ADVOCATE'S GEOCACHE (Book 7)

THE ADVOCATE'S HOMICIDES (Book 8)

THE ADVOCATE'S ILLUSION (Book 9)

THE ADVOCATE'S JUSTICE (Book 10)

THE TUPER SERIES

THE ADVOCATE'S FELONY
(Book 6 of The Advocate Series)

MASON'S MISSING
(First in The Tuper Mystery Series)

CHILDREN'S BOOKS

GASPAR THE FLATULATING GHOST

GASPAR THE FLATULATING GHOST
MEETS A BULLY

GASPAR THE FLATULATING GHOST
FLIES A KITE